# Historic England

# Nonconformist Places of Worship

## Introductions to Heritage Assets

# Summary

Historic England's Introductions to Heritage Assets (IHAs) are accessible, authoritative, illustrated summaries of what we know about specific types of archaeological site, building, landscape or marine asset. Typically they deal with subjects which lack such a summary. This can either be where the literature is dauntingly voluminous, or alternatively where little has been written. Most often it is the latter, and many IHAs bring understanding of site or building types which are neglected or little understood. Many of these are what might be thought of as 'new heritage', that is they date from after the Second World War.

'Nonconformist' has long been used as a description of Protestant Christians in England and Wales who were not part of the Church of England.  Among the numerous denominations are the Baptists, Methodists, Quakers and the Salvation Army. By the mid-nineteenth century their chapels and meeting houses, the subject of this brief introduction, outnumbered the buildings of the Church of England's. While many chapels are now disused or have seen conversion, they remain characteristic and often notable buildings in settlements in all parts of the country.

This guidance note has been written by Christopher Wakeling and edited by Paul Stamper.

It is one is of several guidance documents that can be accessed at HistoricEngland.org.uk/listing/selection-criteria/listing-selection/ihas-buildings/

Published by Historic England August 2016.
All images © Historic England unless otherwise stated.

HistoricEngland.org.uk/listing/selection-criteria/

**Front cover**
The large granite Wesleyan chapel of 1843 at Ponsanooth (Cornwall) dominates this former industrial village, known for its gunpowder mills. Listed  Grade II*.

# Contents

# Introduction

From small country chapels with a few rows of benches, a pulpit and harmonium, to the great city chapels with encircling galleries, rostrum-pulpits and mighty organs, Nonconformist places of worship have made an important contribution to English life for more than three centuries.

The term Nonconformist came to be used as a description of those Protestant Christians in England and Wales who were not part of the Church of England. In the seventeenth and eighteenth centuries such people had frequently been called Dissenters, and by the start of the twentieth century they often chose to describe themselves collectively as Free Churchmen. Among the numerous Nonconformist denominations are the Baptists, Methodists, Quakers and Salvation Army (Fig 1).

In this document, the word chapel is sometimes used generically to refer to all places of Nonconformist worship. Until the twentieth century, Nonconformist places of worship were mostly known as chapels or meeting houses, although many other names were introduced for

**Figure 1**
The meeting house at Jordans (Buckinghamshire) was built in 1688 for a group of Quakers who had met for worship in the nearby farm during the years of persecution. Quakers were especially likely to have their own burial grounds, and among those buried here is William Penn, the founder of Pennsylvania. Listed Grade I.

**Figure 2**
The bold artisan-Baroque façade of this Independent meeting house (now called Old Meeting) in Norwich shows the confidence with which some Nonconformists built after 1689. Dating from 1693, it exemplifies the classic 'long-wall' façade arrangement, and its two tiers of windows reflect the galleried interior. Listed Grade I.

**Figure 3**
Although now Unitarian, Mary Street chapel, Taunton (Somerset), was built – probably in 1721 – for a Baptist congregation. Such interiors had much in common with Anglican churches of the day, although Nonconformists were more likely to have a central block of seating rather than a central gangway. Listed Grade II*.

particular types, such as tabernacles, gospel halls, citadels and central halls. More recent examples are quite likely to be referred to as churches. Commonly, facilities for educational and social activities are provided, as well as space for worship.

It is sometimes thought that Nonconformist chapels are principally a northern phenomenon, but this is misleading: they are (or were) as common a feature of Cheltenham or Cornwall as of Leeds or Lancashire. Individual denominations have not been equally strong in all parts of the country, but by the Victorian era almost every town had a good number of Nonconformist places, and even quite small villages or scattered settlements might boast one or two chapels as alternatives to the parish church (Fig 3). Indeed, since the mid-nineteenth century the Church of England's buildings have been outnumbered by the Nonconformists'.

Yet, because the study of English religious architecture traditionally focused on Anglican churches, Nonconformist buildings (along with those of the Roman Catholics, Jews and other faiths) have often been overlooked or poorly understood. Recent research has tended to widen the scope, but a serious imbalance of knowledge and appreciation persists. Buildings from the early periods of Nonconformist history (the seventeenth and eighteenth centuries) have been best documented, and those from subsequent centuries are least well studied. Most of the major Nonconformist denominations have shared in the general decline of church-going over the past half century, but their buildings have been disproportionately vulnerable to demolition or inappropriate adaptation.

# 1 Historical Background and Chronology

## 1.1   The seventeenth century

Nonconformists emerged from the unstable religious world of the English Reformation. Three denominations – Presbyterians, Independents (or Congregationalists) and Baptists – can trace their origins to the sixteenth century, but the need for their own places of worship did not commonly arise until after the 1662 Act of Uniformity, when

**Figure 4**
John Wesley's 'New Room', in Bristol, was the Methodists' first purpose-built chapel; begun in 1739 and greatly enlarged in 1748. Above the chapel are the rooms where Wesley and other travelling preachers stayed. The building, which was comprehensively restored in 1929-30, is now being extended to provide further facilities for visitors and researchers. Listed Grade I.

about two thousand ministers were ejected from the Church of England. Nonconformists were then driven underground by successive legislation, especially the Conventicle Act of 1664 and the Five Mile Act of 1665. Despite severe persecution the newly-formed Quakers did build in those years, and they were briefly joined by other denominations following the short-lived Declarations of Indulgence of 1672 and 1687, which suspended penal laws against those who worshipped outside the Church of England (Fig 1). Only with the 1689 Act of Toleration was there a permanent change, when freedom of worship was extended to all but Roman Catholics and Unitarians. Thousands of places of worship were registered by Nonconformists in the twenty years after 1689; mostly houses and other secular buildings, but including dozens of places that were either specially built or permanently adapted for religious use.

## 1.2   The coming of Methodism

During the middle part of the eighteenth century Methodism emerged, initially as an evangelical movement inside the Church of England, and with John Wesley and George Whitefield as its most famous leaders. Despite its success in reaching large numbers of people who were not committed Christians, the new movement was viewed with suspicion by the Church of England.

Denied access to many Anglican pulpits, Wesley established a network of preaching houses, although his followers were initially expected to attend their parish churches for communion (Fig 4). Ultimately, however, Methodism separated from the Church of England and swelled the Nonconformist ranks. Its campaign of spiritual renewal, which also helped revive the fortunes of Baptists and Congregationalists, resulted in a formidable building programme. More than 1,300 new chapels opened in the second half of the eighteenth century, besides a far greater number of more makeshift places of Nonconformist worship (Fig 5).

## 1.3 Nineteenth-century developments

Methodism was adept at working in those areas where the Church of England was weakest: burgeoning towns and industrial districts, and among the rural poor. In the early nineteenth century its membership soared, boosted in part by breakaway groups (such as the Primitive Methodists) who appealed to particular classes or localities. Between 1800 and 1850, new chapels were opened at the extraordinary rate of almost 250 each year. Methodists led the field, but several of the older denominations played a significant role, and the government's million-pound grant (in 1818) to build new Anglican churches was largely a response to the Nonconformists' prodigious success.

Throughout the Victorian era the major Nonconformist denominations continued to grow very steadily, with an ambitious programme of chapel-building. Many villages gained their first purpose-built chapel in those years, and most towns and cities gained new chapels in conspicuous locations. The Church of England was by then busily erecting new churches, but could never match the sheer number of Nonconformist premises.

The nineteenth century witnessed a very gradual easing of the legislation which had continued to restrict Nonconformists. Laws which excluded all but practising Anglicans from government and

**Figures 5 (top) and 6 (bottom)**
(Top)John Wesley's spiritual and social vision was much influenced by his contact with the Moravian church. This Moravian chapel (of 1784-5) at Fairfield, east of Manchester, is at the heart of an extensive settlement which the Moravians began in 1783. The basic design was one of the first works by Benjamin Latrobe, whose father was a Moravian minister. Listed Grade II*.

(Bottom) Dating from 1820, just seven years after Unitarians were granted freedom of worship, the Unitarian chapel in Brighton, East Sussex (by the local architect, A.H. Wilds) is a striking example of the Greek revival. Listed Grade II.

**Figure 7**
Old Chapel (Unitarian) in Dukinfield, Greater Manchester, was built in 1839-40 to the designs of Richard Tattersall. Within a Gothic framework, its high pulpit and galleries re-affirm the centrality of preaching in the Protestant tradition. Listed Grade II*.

municipal posts were repealed in 1828-9, and in 1871 it became illegal to debar Nonconformists from teaching or studying in English universities. Unitarians gained freedom of worship in 1813, and the Dissenters' Chapels Act (of 1844) effectively secured for them those chapels in which they had worshipped for the past twenty-five (Fig 3). After 1836 Nonconformists had the right to conduct marriage ceremonies, and in 1880 they were granted the right to conduct burial services in parish churchyards.

Towards the end of the nineteenth century, as wealthier families moved to the suburbs, Nonconformists made a special effort to reach the remaining urban poor: the citadels of the newly-founded Salvation Army became familiar landmarks, Methodists built central halls, and even Quakers established missions. The provision of social facilities and schoolrooms, which had long been a notable element of larger chapels, was especially important at that time.

## 1.4 Twentieth-century changes

It was in the Edwardian era that the Nonconformist denominations were at their largest and most influential. Thereafter, with membership numbers generally in decline, there was some consolidation of forces. As early as 1907, ecumenical negotiations led to the creation of the United Methodist Church (combining three strands of Methodism), and in 1932 that body joined with the larger Wesleyan and Primitive connexions to form the Methodist Church. Similarly, the United Reformed Church was created in 1972 (uniting the Presbyterian Church of England and most Congregational churches). Such mainstream groups continued to build new places of worship in particular situations, but overall reduced the number of their buildings.

By way of contrast, many newer denominations experienced growth. Christian Science spread to Britain from America at the start of the twentieth century, while the Church of Jesus Christ of Latter-day Saints (the Mormons) and Jehovah's Witnesses greatly increased their presence in Britain during the second half of the century (Fig 16). Each of these groups has developed distinctive types of building. Even more significant recently has been the rise of Pentecostal churches, many of which have needed large buildings to accommodate their growing congregations.

**Figure 8**
Centenary Wesleyan chapel, York, was built in 1839-40 (to the designs of James Simpson) to mark the first hundred years of Methodism. With its encircling gallery, wide-spanned ceiling and set-piece of organ, pulpit and communion table it seems to typify grand Methodist interiors of the time. Originally, however, the ground floor was more fully pewed and a narrower pulpit rose almost to gallery level. Listed Grade II*.

# 2 Development of the Building Type

## 2.1 Early examples

From the late seventeenth century onwards, most purpose-built chapels and meeting houses (and many adapted premises) were rectangular buildings, generally entered in one of the long sides and with a high pulpit in the centre of the opposite long wall, where it might be framed by a pair of tall windows (Fig 2). Characteristically, there would be a central block of benches or box pews facing the pulpit, with further seating (sometimes tiered) around the sides of the building. Larger buildings would very commonly have galleries, to keep congregations within sight and sound of the pulpit (Fig 4). Communion tables would be immediately in front of the pulpit or in a central table-pew, and

**Figure 9**
The 2,500-seat Westminster Chapel was built in 1863-5 for the congregation of Samuel Martin, one of the great preachers of the day. Two tiers of galleries and radial ground-floor pews emphasise the chapel's curved plan. Using cast-iron, the architect (W. F. Poulton) was able to provide virtually uninterrupted views of the preacher's rostrum. Listed Grade II.

**Figure 10**
Umberslade Baptist church, near Hockley Heath in Warwickshire (built in 1877 to the designs of George Ingall), was financed by G.F. Muntz of Umberslade Hall. Its tower contains a set of eight bells. Since the building closed for regular services it has been taken into care by the Historic Chapels Trust. Listed Grade II*.

Baptists might have a baptistery pool beneath the floor. Quakers, with no need for pulpits, communion table or baptisteries, had a simpler arrangement of benches facing a raised stand: where possible, their meeting houses were arranged to provide separate accommodation for the women's business meetings. Many early chapels and meeting-houses were relatively plain, sometimes vernacular, but quite elaborate architectural treatment was possible, and important fittings were often of high quality. In a very few instances unusual plan-forms were adopted by Presbyterians: T-shaped and cruciform examples are known, and later, octagonal and elliptical chapels were built.

## 2.2 Eighteenth-century buildings

The new religious movements of the eighteenth century varied this pattern of building a little. George Whitefield, the charismatic Calvinistic Methodist preacher, attracted such a following that a series of so-called tabernacles was erected for him, square chapels each reportedly large enough for several thousand hearers. John Wesley's more numerous preaching houses were rarely so large, but his major buildings often provided space for a range of educational and social facilities as well as worship Wesley, having admired the fine eight-sided Presbyterian chapel of 1753-6 in Norwich, erected a clutch of octagonal chapels in the 1760s and 70s, though otherwise stayed with rectangular plans. When he accepted the need to provide communion facilities in Methodist buildings, a recess for the communion table was sometimes created behind the pulpit. By the later eighteenth century, Nonconformists began to favour short-wall façades – particularly in towns where street frontages were at a premium – with a correspondingly long internal axis. Stylistically, the prevailing tastes of the day were employed: sub-Baroque features around 1700, giving way later to Anglo-Palladian and then Neoclassical habits, and with a sub-theme of Gothic designs first appearing in the 1750s.

## 2.3 Early nineteenth-century chapels

During the great burst of chapel-building in the first decades of the nineteenth century, the design of large urban chapels was refined. Encircling galleries (usually on cast-iron columns) began to supersede the straight-fronted kind, and wherever possible interiors were spanned without interruption. Organs gradually came to replace bands of musicians, and were often placed very prominently at gallery level behind the pulpit; this being most common in major Methodist chapels. A large Sunday-school hall might be provided, sometimes at the rear or (if the site allowed) below the main chapel space. Short-wall façades became most common, although the long-wall pattern persisted, especially for small rural chapels, and polygonal plans were used for some urban sites. Gothic continued to be chosen by a minority of Nonconformists throughout the early nineteenth century. In line with the architectural tendencies of the period, however, classicism was more widely used, sometimes without columns but often with ambitious Greek or Roman characteristics. (Fig 6). Towards mid-century, bell-towers became a little more usual and by the 1840s some larger Gothic chapels were built with a full repertoire of spires and structural side aisles. The Unitarians showed a particular taste for Gothic.

**Figure 11**
This small chapel was built in 1863 for the Bible Christians (a Methodist body that was rooted in south-west England) in the mining community of Wheal Busy (Cornwall). It has a 'long-wall' façade, rather than the gable-end frontage which was becoming more popular. Listed Grade II*.

Leading architects undertook a number of important Nonconformist commissions, but a significant role was played by denominational specialists, such as the Wesleyan Methodists' William Jenkins and James Simpson or the Congregationalists' James Fenton (Fig 8). Very few chapel interiors from the early nineteenth century survive intact. Large chapels have been particularly susceptible to change. Pulpits (almost as high as the gallery in larger buildings) were generally lowered, and sometimes adapted or replaced by rostrum-pulpits, while ground-floor seating was often modified or replaced when upright-backed box pews fell from favour.

## 2.4 High Victorian chapel architecture

The Nonconformists' sustained building campaign of the High Victorian years produced a great variety of chapels. From these years date many of the surviving small chapels in villages and urban backstreets, which are likely to have gable-end façades, perhaps decoratively treated, although the long-wall entry type persisted in some country districts (Fig 11). Prefabricated iron chapels ('tin tabernacles') were also used, sometimes as a temporary expedient. For medium-to-large chapels the gable-end façade remained a common feature, and could be treated in any of the then-current architectural styles: classical, Renaissance, Romanesque or Gothic. Gothic chapels of a more elaborate kind were frequently built in these years, mostly retaining a central pulpit and communion table, and minimising the use of stone columns that would interfere with sightlines. For similar reasons, central blocks of pews, not central gangways, remained usual in larger chapels regardless of style, and it became common to have floors that sloped down to the pulpit area.

Much thought was given to the use of plan-forms that fostered congregational worship, and some very striking designs were created using fan-shaped, oval, polygonal and cross-in-square arrangements, rather as was happening in continental Protestantism (Fig 9). A number of enormous city chapels were built for charismatic

**Figures 12 (top) and 13 (bottom)**
(Top) The small Primitive Methodist chapel at Fulmodeston (Norfolk) was extended and refitted in 1902 by a local builder. Its broad pews placed the congregation directly in front of the pulpit and communion table, and a harmonium (just out of view on the left) accompanied the singing.

(Bottom) Westgate Hall, Newcastle upon Tyne (1901-2, designed by Crouch and Butler) is one of the central halls that were built by Wesleyans around 1900 in an attempt to attract the urban poor. Resolutely un-churchlike in appearance, it incorporates shops at street level and a large first-floor hall. Listed Grade II.

**Figure 14**

Nonconformist themes inspired these windows (completed 1912 by Abbot and Co. to designs by Charles Elliot) in what is now the United Reformed Church at, Fairhaven (Lancashire). The largest panel shows the departure of the Pilgrim Fathers, while among the eight Nonconformists depicted above are Milton, George Fox, Bunyan and Wesley. Listed Grade II*.

preachers; Spurgeon's Metropolitan Tabernacle in Southwark being the most famous. In crowded urban situations, Nonconformists were able to make effective use of valuable sites because it was hardly ever felt necessary to face east. The provision of school and social facilities was still a priority, and semi-basement halls were created for these purposes where land was limited. In this period all but the smallest chapels were architect-designed, generally by local practitioners or by one of the dozens of Nonconformist specialists. Among those specialists were Joseph James, John Tarring, George Bidlake, James Wilson, W. F. Poulton and James Cubitt, although many other influential figures could be mentioned.

## 2.5 Chapels and mission buildings: c1890-1914

By the end of the nineteenth century the era of prosperous urban chapels was beginning to pass, as the middle classes moved to the suburbs. During the late Victorian and Edwardian years, well-crafted chapels were built for middle-class congregations – perhaps just outside a town centre if not in the suburbs – but rarely on the previous scale; galleries were often deemed unnecessary. In some places long vistas and chancels (and thus off-centre pulpits) were favoured; in others compact plans were used, combined with a pattern of curved pews to focus attention on the pulpit area. Gothic or Arts and Crafts styles tended to predominate, generally with high-quality fittings and sometimes with enterprising details. Referring to such suburban chapels, Pevsner wrote of the 'the much gayer and livelier, and in point of fact remarkably up-to-date, style which characterizes chapels about 1900 and is almost absent from churches.'

By contrast, Gothic was routinely avoided for the various types of building that were intended to appeal to the poorer urban classes. The Salvation Army had its trademark brick forts; the Methodists invested in a generation of grand mission buildings (including the Wesleyans' central halls) to rival commercial theatres; and many of the older denominations built institutes and other outreach centres on determinedly un-ecclesiastical lines (Fig 13). Mission buildings might have to double as concert halls, gymnasiums or soup kitchens as well as places of worship, so that movable chairs were the norm. Most central halls had tip-up seats. Novel means of financing were devised: central halls usually incorporated shops at street level, and many ordinary chapels of this era have lines of masonry with the initials of supporters who had collected or donated for the building fund.

**Figure 15**
The top-lit internal wall of the Baptist church at Waterlooville, Hampshire (of 1966-7, by Michael Manser Associates) provides a dramatic backdrop to the dais with its wide pulpit, communion table and (right) open baptismal pool.

The architectural practices of George Baines, Joseph Crouch, W. A. Gelder and Gordon & Gunton were among those that specialised in Nonconformist work in the early twentieth century, and important contributions were made by less specialist architects such as Edgar Wood and Morley Horder.

## 2.6 Nonconformist buildings between the wars

After 1914 the Edwardian habits of suburban chapel-building continued, although Gothic gradually fell from favour, giving way to a taste for Romanesque and neo-Georgian features. Often the scale was more modest than before. One occasionally finds a hall – the first stage of an intended suite of chapel buildings – still serving for worship, Sunday school and social events. Inner-city missions and central halls also continued to be built well into the age of the cinema, and using up-to-date commercial styles. A few interesting city-centre chapels were created when a congregation, displaced by retail or office developments, had the initiative and the funds to commission an adventurous design. The influence of Expressionism, Scandinavian motifs or Art Deco can be seen in places. Some architects (for instance, William Hayne, F. W. Lawrence and Smee & Houchin) worked regularly for Nonconformists, but there was less opportunity for specialisation than in the previous century.

## 2.7 Chapel-building since 1945

During the decades after the 1939-45 war, Nonconformists led the way in the development of what were sometimes called church centres; that is, places of worship with a range of social and educational facilities. On housing estates or in inner-city districts, new chapels might thus accommodate clinics, youth clubs, adult education and amateur dramatics as well as Sunday schools and services. Modern architectural forms and materials were frequently employed. In the fifties and sixties, concrete

**Figure 16**
Since the 1950s the Church of Jesus Christ of Latter-day Saints (popularly known as the Mormons) has built meeting houses in most parts of England. This example at Lawley, Telford, Shropshire (of 2004-5, by McBains Cooper), characteristically features a neat spire.

frames, partnered with brick walling, were commonly used. Contemporary European church architecture – both expressionist and more reticent kinds – influenced many new chapels. Centralised and linear plan-forms were used, and communion tables often occupied an axial position, with a low pulpit to one side. One of the most influential Nonconformist architects of the post-war era was Edward Mills, a Methodist.

Through the seventies and eighties the range of architectural influences developed: brickwork in the style of Aalto or Louis Kahn was common, less often board-marked concrete or sleek steel and glass (Fig 15). A growing desire for the flexible use of space led to the use of chairs, rather than fixed seating, and it was not unusual to have a moveable lectern/pulpit and communion table. Somewhat separate from these trends, the Mormons and Jehovah's Witnesses undertook a steady programme of construction, the Mormon buildings often being distinguished by tall spires or spikes and a relatively traditional layout of fixed seating, while the Witnesses' kingdom halls were more understated. Both groups also have a small number of larger, more elaborate, buildings (temples and assembly halls, respectively).

In the decades around the millennium the traditional Nonconformist denominations, sometimes working in ecumenical partnerships, commissioned some striking buildings. Octagonal plans enjoyed a certain revival, for instance in the Salvation Army, which replaced many of its older citadels. Pentecostalists and some other evangelical groups who had previously been inclined to use adapted premises erected a few large and positively un-churchlike buildings with family-friendly facilities and full use of modern technology in the worship area.

# 3 Associations

The majority of congregations will not have originated in their present premises. In places where clergy were ejected from the parish church (or, indeed, cathedral) in 1662, the relationship between that building and any consequent Nonconformist chapel may be of interest. It may also be fruitful to consider the places – such as guild halls, warehouses and farm buildings – in which Nonconformists gathered during the years of persecution. From later centuries, too, most bodies have an early history of meeting in borrowed accommodation (or even the open air) before being able to erect a place of worship. The cottage in which a group of Primitive Methodist farm labourers first met, or the schoolroom in which a fellowship of Caribbean immigrants initially came together for Pentecostal worship, will be of significance, even if not necessarily of architectural importance. In the case of the Baptists and other denominations who practise full immersion, it may be that natural baptismal sites – rivers, the sea, lakes – were a key feature of a congregation's history.

The curtilage of a chapel always repays attention. Although some chapels open directly onto a road or street, the majority will have had enough space to create at least a forecourt which provides a formal approach to the chapel, commonly with walls or railings and gates. There may also be original paving or planted areas, and occasionally historic light fittings survive. A good proportion of early chapels and meeting houses had their own burial grounds, sometimes even preceding the date of building. These, along with any memorials inside a chapel, provide important evidence for the history of the congregations involved. War memorials are generally of even wider community significance. (The paired Nonconformist and Anglican chapels found in most municipal or private cemeteries from the nineteenth century rarely have associations with any individual congregation, however.)

Some people are always likely to have travelled long distances to their chosen chapel. The poor will generally have walked, but stables, cart sheds and mounting blocks remain at a few old chapels, as evidence of how some others arrived. Later, of course, public transport routes and then road access and space for car parking affected the location of many urban chapels. Very many Nonconformist places of worship have contiguous school rooms and social facilities. Where larger buildings do not have such facilities on hand, it may be that a former chapel, some distance away, was retained for those purposes. Historically the group of chapel buildings was often adjoined by the minister's house (or manse), but since the Victorian years such proximity has become less usual.

Sometimes a chapel stands within view of a building that has been its *raison d'être*. In rural places it might be the big house in which a patron of the chapel lived, while in industrial townships it might be the factory whose owners provided the chapel for their employees.

In a wider context, most Nonconformists will be familiar with a national network of denominational sites. Quakers, for instance, feel a special connection with Swarthmoor Hall (Cumbria) and other places in north-west England where George Fox's message found a receptive audience; they also know of the major Quaker boarding schools, the residential adult college at Bournville in Birmingham, and their 'headquarters' building (Friends House) on Euston Road in London. Comparable maps can be drawn up for every Nonconformist body, and indeed some denominations have heritage trails around the country. Sites associated with movements that originated in Britain (including the Methodists, Quakers and Salvation Army) are particularly likely to be of international interest.

# 4 Change and the Future

During the past fifty years many chapels have closed. Urban examples have been most vulnerable to demolition, while smaller rural examples have often been adapted for residential use or agricultural purposes. Latterly more instances of sensitive adaptation for commercial or public use have been seen, and in some parts of the country closed chapels have been taken on by different religious groups (sometimes of other faiths). In 1993 the Historic Chapels Trust was created to take custody of a selection of closed, non-Anglican places of worship that are of particular historic or architectural importance (Fig 17). Parallel with these developments, chapels that continue in use have commonly been altered to provide improved community facilities or to allow for more flexible forms of worship.

Current forecasts are that many of the traditional Nonconformist denominations in England (including the Methodists, Congregationalists, Unitarians and United Reformed Church) will continue to decline, so that a significant number of historic chapels is likely to close. This decline may be offset by a continued growth among Pentecostal and other newer denominations, probably with varied architectural results: some such groups have skilfully adapted older places of worship for their use, while others have converted secular premises or – less commonly – built afresh.

**Figure 17**
Bethesda Methodist New Connexion chapel, Hanley, Stoke-on-Trent (as altered in 1859 by Robert Scrivener), which closed in 1985, is now in the care of the Historic Chapels Trust. Listed Grade II*.

Several challenges face those concerned for the future of historic Nonconformist buildings. One is the need to assess the importance of interior fittings, at a time when the retention of fixed seating, pulpits and organs is questioned by many worshippers. A wider task is to understand to relative significance of thousands of buildings that have been little studied, particularly when so many may be subject to possible change or demolition. And for those Nonconformist buildings that have no future as places of worship, there remains the challenge of finding new uses that respect the historic fabric (Fig 18).

**Figure 18**

In about 1970 Square Congregational chapel, Halifax (West Yorkshire), was closed for worship. Soon a series of fires destroyed most of the mid-Victorian 'miniature cathedral' (seen on the left), while its 1772 predecessor (the back of which is seen here) steadily decayed. In 1988 a local Trust began to stabilise the earlier building (listed Grade II*), using it as an arts centre. An extension, now under construction, will add a second auditorium.

# 5 Further Reading

Introductory accounts of the subject can be found in John Betjeman, *First and Last Loves*, 1952 (pages 90-119, 'Nonconformist Architecture') and David A. Barton, *Discovering Chapels and Meeting Houses*, (1975). Late in 2016, or in 2017, Historic England will publish Christopher Wakeling's new overview, *Chapels of England*.

Very much more substantial are the four extensively-illustrated volumes of Christopher Stell's *Inventory of Nonconformist Chapels and Meeting-houses* (*…in Central England*, 1986; *…in South-West England*, 1991; *… in the North of England*, 1994; and *…in Eastern England*, 2002), which systematically describe virtually all surviving Nonconformist places of worship from before 1800, as well as a good selection of later examples.

Among several denominational studies, the most important are George W. Dolbey, *The Architectural Expression of Methodism* (1964); Graham and Judy Hague, *The Unitarian Heritage* (1986), and David M. Butler, *The Quaker Meeting Houses of Britain*, 1999) (2 vols.).

Regional and local surveys have contributed much to the understanding of chapels, and useful examples include David and Susan Neave, *East Riding Chapels and Meeting Houses* (1990); Nigel Temple, *Islington Chapels* (1992); Janet Ede, Norma Virgoe and Tom Williamson, *Halls of Zion: Chapels and Meeting-Houses in Norfolk* (1994); Rosalind Kaye, *Chapels in Essex* (1999); and Jeremy Lake, Jo Cox and Eric Berry, *Diversity and Vitality: The Methodist and Nonconformist Chapels of Cornwall* (2001). Countless individual chapel histories have been published locally.

Nineteenth-century topics are introduced in Chris Brooks and Andrew Saint (eds.), *The Victorian Church* (1995) (pages 82-97, 'The Nonconformist Traditions'), and Bridget Cherry (ed.), *Dissent and the Gothic Revival* (2007). The Chapels Society (website: chapelssociety.org.uk) has a programme of events and publications: in 2013 it produced *Sitting in Chapel*, a volume dealing with historic seating in Nonconformist places of worship.

Several Nonconformist denominations have history societies and/or archives, and Dr Williams's Library (14 Gordon Square, London WC1H 0AR; website: dwlib.co.uk) is a major resource for the study of Nonconformist history.

## 5.1 Contact Historic England

### East Midlands
2nd Floor, Windsor House
Cliftonville
Northampton NN1 5BE
Tel: 01604 735460
Email: eastmidlands@HistoricEngland.org.uk

### East of England
Brooklands
24 Brooklands Avenue
Cambridge CB2 8BU
Tel: 01223 582749
Email: eastofengland@HistoricEngland.org.uk

### Fort Cumberland
Fort Cumberland Road
Eastney
Portsmouth PO4 9LD
Tel: 023 9285 6704
Email: fort.cumberland@HistoricEngland.org.uk

### London
1 Waterhouse Square
138-142 Holborn
London EC1N 2ST
Tel: 020 7973 3700
Email: london@HistoricEngland.org.uk

### North East
Bessie Surtees House
41-44 Sandhill
Newcastle Upon Tyne
NE1 3JF
Tel: 0191 269 1255
Email: northeast@HistoricEngland.org.uk

### North West
3rd Floor, Canada House
3 Chepstow Street
Manchester M1 5FW
Tel: 0161 242 1416
Email: northwest@HistoricEngland.org.uk

### South East
Eastgate Court
195-205 High Street
Guildford GU1 3EH
Tel: 01483 252020
Email: southeast@HistoricEngland.org.uk

### South West
29 Queen Square
Bristol BS1 4ND
Tel: 0117 975 1308
Email: southwest@HistoricEngland.org.uk

### Swindon
The Engine House
Fire Fly Avenue
Swindon  SN2 2EH
Tel: 01793 445050
Email: swindon@HistoricEngland.org.uk

### West Midlands
The Axis
10 Holliday Street
Birmingham B1 1TG
Tel: 0121 625 6870
Email: westmidlands@HistoricEngland.org.uk

### Yorkshire
37 Tanner Row
York YO1 6WP
Tel: 01904 601948
Email: yorkshire@HistoricEngland.org.uk

# 6 Acknowledgements

## Images

**© Historic England**

Figure 1: DP160125

Figure 2: DP160220

Figure 3: DP166303

Figure 4: DP166243

Figure 6: DP165334

Figure 7: DP143748

Figure 8: DP181099

Figure 9: DP155982

Figure 10: DP157555

Figure 11: DP160702

Figure 12: DP160461

Figure 13 DP157035

Figure 14: DP156986

Figure 15: DP160444

Figure 16: DP166327

Figure 17: DP143793

**© Other**

Front cover: Eric Berry

Figure 5: David Dixon

Every effort has been made to trace the copyright holders and we apologise in advance for any unintentional omissions, which we would be pleased to correct in any subsequent editions.

This page is left blank intentionally

We are the public body that looks after England's historic environment. We champion historic places, helping people understand, value and care for them.

Please contact
guidance@HistoricEngland.org.uk
with any questions about this document.

HistoricEngland.org.uk

If you would like this document in a different format, please contact our customer services department on:

Tel: 0370 333 0607
Fax: 01793 414926
Textphone: 0800 015 0174
Email: customers@HistoricEngland.org.uk

All information and weblinks accurate at the time of publication.

Please consider the environment before printing this document

HEAG139
Publication date: August 2016 © Historic England
Design: Historic England

Printed in Great Britain
by Amazon